Calvary Assembly of God Joy Club

Hey Good Lookin'

What You Got Cookin'?

JEANNIE FELLER

Hey Good Lookin'

Copyright © 2024 Jeannie Feller. All rights reserved.

No rights claimed for public domain material, all rights reserved. No parts of this publication may be reproduced, stored in any retrieval system, or transmitted in any form or by any means, electronic, mechanical, recording, or otherwise, without the prior written permission of the author. Violations may be subject to civil or criminal penalties.

ISBN:
978-1-63308-758-3 Hardback Color interior
978-1-63308-759-0 Soft Cover with Color interior
978-1-63308-760-6 Soft Cover with Black and White Interior
978-1-63308-761-3 Ebook

Calvary Assembly of God Joy Club

Cover and Interior Design by *R'tor John D. Maghuyop*

CHALFANT ECKERT
PUBLISHING

PO Box 1665, Rolla MO 65402

Printed in United States of America

Calvary Assembly of God Joy Club

Hey Good Lookin'

What You Got Cookin'?

JEANNIE FELLER

Table of Contents

Dedication 7
In Loving Memory 9
Pastor Kemp's Favorite Chili Frito Surprise 10
Jean's Favorite One Pan Banana Bread 11
Chili Champs 12

Soups and Salads

Cheeseburger Soup 14
Cheesy Potato Soup 15
Crazy Good Salad 16
Potato Soup 17
Taco Salad 18
Tomato Basil Soup 19
Tomato Tortellini Soup 20
Spiral Noodle Pasta Salad 21
World's Best Buttermilk Ranch Dressing 22

Meats and Main Dishes

Baked Noodles in Parmesan Sauce 24
Baked Peppers with Meat – Sharon Style 25
Beachcomber Casserole 26
Chicken Packets 27
Chow Mein 28
Crock Pot Ranch Pork Chops 29
Hamburger Stew 30
Lebanon Summer Sausage 31
One Pot Beef Roast and Vegetable Dinner 32
Party Meatballs 33
Sloppy Joes 34
Steak Marinade 35
Stuffed Peppers 36
Tuscan Chicken 37
Zucchini Casserole 38

Side Dishes

Barbecued Sauerkraut 40
Cabbage Cheese Casserole 41
Cabbage Casserole 42
Cheese Cauliflower 43
Cheesy Hash Browns 44
Corn Casserole 45
Creamy Cauliflower Bake 46
Hot Yeast Rolls 47
Houston House Rolls 48
Perfect Dill Pickles 49
Scotch Eggs 50
Shoepeg Corn Casserole 51

Desserts

Apple Crumb Pie 54
Apple Dapple Cake 55
Banana Nut Bread 56
Blackberry Cream Cheese Pie 57
Blackberry Dessert 58
Chocolate Chip Cookie Dough
to Eat Raw 59
Coconut Cream Cake 60
Coffee Punch 61
Crack Cake 62
Cranberry Chip Cookies 63
Creamy Blueberry Gelatin Salad 64
Deluxe Oatmeal Raisin Cookies 65
Dessert Pizza 66
Easy Pineapple Casserole 67
Easy Sugar Free Chocolate Pie 68
Fruit Pizza 69
Gluten-Free Orange Bundt Cake 70
Gluten-Free Oreo Bundt Cake 71
Hawaiian Cheesecake 72
Lazy Man's Peach Cobbler 73
Lucky 7 Pie Crust 74
Maple Syrup by Scratch 75
Million Dollar Pie 76
Old Fashion Yellow Cookies 77
Orange Dream-Sickle Salad 78
Pastor Brian's Pumpkin Bars 79
Pumpkin Pie Squares 80
Red Velvet Crinkles 81
Sopapilla Cheescake Bars 82
Sweet Cinnamon Biscuits 83
Truffles 84
Zuccini Bread 85

Calvary Cherubs

Calvary's Cherubs Cook

Aidynn Noilges (Age 10)..............89
Lakota Moentmann (Age 8)...........89
Echo Moentmann (Age 6) 90
Isaac Baggett (Age 11) 90
Emma Hodge (Age 10) 91
William Cottner (Age 4)................91
Lilly Demire (Age 11) 92
Cheryl Holtmeyer (Age 12) 92
Aaron Hodge (Age 8)..................93
Henry Mendenhall (Age 9 ½) 93
Harper Light (Age 9)...................93
Payton Light (Age 7) 94
Paisley Degroat (Age 7)................94

Recipe For Life

JESUS IS..96

Dedication

This cookbook is dedicated to the lovely ladies of Calvary Assembly of God Church who so lovingly step forward to keep our kitchen open and thriving whatever the occasion may be.

Special thanks go to Sharon Tennyson, Janice Dodson, Sharon Warren, Mary Ann Rosenberg and Cheryl Baggett who so often give their time and donate the necessary ingredients. And if I've left you out, please forgive my omission and accept our sincere gratitude.

Our appreciation goes out to Janice Dodson who took the cover photo. We don't see you there, but your pictures are the best! Thank you for sharing.

And a BIG THANK YOU to everyone who Contributed a recipe. GOD BLESS YOU ALL for making the cookbook the success that it is.

In Loving Memory

This cookbook wouldn't be complete without favorite recipes from our former Pastor, M. Danny Kemp, and his wife Jean who lovingly served this congregation until our HEAVENLY FATHER called them home.

Pastor Kemp's Favorite Chili Frito Surprise

INGREDIENTS

3 cups Frito Chips

2 cups shredded cheddar cheese

1 can chili

DIRECTIONS

Preheat oven to 350 degrees.

In an 8" x 11" glass baking dish, line the bottom with corn chips.

Cover with half the chili.

Top with half the cheddar cheese.

Repeat both layers.

Bake for 30 minutes.

Jean's Favorite One Pan Banana Bread

INGREDIENTS

1/3 cup vegetable oil

2 1/3 cups Bisquick

1 ½ cup mashed ripe bananas

1 cup sugar

½ teaspoon vanilla

½ cup chopped nuts

3 eggs

DIRECTIONS

Preheat oven to 350 degrees.

Generously grease bottom of 9" x 5" x 3" baking pan.

Stir all ingredients in the pan with a fork until moistened.

Beat vigorously for 1 minute.

Bake 55 - 60 minutes.

Chili Champs

And what cookbook would be complete without a good chili recipe.

Congratulations to Janet and Kenneth Ragsdell for being the First-Place winners in the Annual Chili Cookoff in February.

Your chili was awesome.

Cheeseburger Soup

INGREDIENTS

1 pound ground beef

¾ cup chopped onion

¾ cup shredded carrots

¾ cup diced celery

1 teaspoon dried basil

1 teaspoon parsley flakes

4 Tablespoons butter (divided)

¼ cup sour cream

3 cups chicken broth

4 cups diced, peeled potatoes

¼ cup all-purpose flour

8 ounces process American cheese

1 ½ cups milk

¾ teaspoon salt

¼ - ½ teaspoon pepper

DIRECTIONS

In a 3-quart saucepan, brown the beef, drain, and set aside.

In the same saucepan, sauté onion, carrots, celery, basil, and parsley in 1 Tablespoon butter until vegetables are tender – about 10 minutes.

Add broth, potatoes, and beef. Bring to a boil, reduce heat, cover and simmer 10 – 12 minutes or until potatoes are tender.

Meanwhile, in a small skillet, melt the remaining butter. Add flour and cook and stir for 3 – 5 minutes or until bubbly.

Add to soup. Bring to a boil. Cook and stir for 2 minutes. Reduce to low. Add cheese, milk, salt, and pepper. Cook until cheese is melted.

Remove from the heat and stir in the sour cream.

Contributed by Sharon Tennyson

Cheesy Potato Soup

INGREDIENTS

2 – 3 carrots, shaved

2 – 3 celery stalks, chopped

1 medium onion, sliced

5 large potatoes, peeled, sliced, and boiled -OR- you can substitute one package frozen diced potatoes

1 large can (46 ounces or so) chicken broth

1 can evaporated milk

1/3 – ½ pound Velvetta cheese

DIRECTIONS

Sauté carrots, celery, and onion in butter till tender.

Add chicken broth to boiled potatoes and sautéed vegetables. Simmer.

Just before serving (5 – 10 minutes before), add one can evaporated milk and Velveeta cheese.

Serve when the cheese is melted.

NOTE: This recipe also makes great broccoli cheese soup. Just use one package frozen broccoli instead of potatoes.

Contributed by Jeannie Feller

Crazy Good Salad

INGREDIENTS

½ head green cabbage cut into thin strips and diced

½ head red cabbage cut into thin strips and diced

1 red onion, diced small

1 yellow bell pepper, diced small

1 large tomato, diced small

1 large green apple, diced

1 cucumber, diced

1 carrot, grated

Dressing:

4 Tablespoons cream cheese, softened

2 Tablespoons mayonnaise

1 Tablespoon mustard

3 cloves garlic

DIRECTIONS

In a mixing bowl, combine cream cheese, mayo, mustard and garlic. Mix well.

Put diced mixture into a serving dish.

Add dressing mixture and combine.

Add 1 teaspoon salt and 1 teaspoon black pepper.

Contributed by Deidra Holtmeyer

Potato Soup

INGREDIENTS

5 slices of bacon, diced

3 Tablespoons olive oil

1 cup diced inions

4 cloves of garlic

¼ cup flour

2 cups chicken stock

2 cups milk

1.5 pounds Yukon potatoes, diced

1 cup shredded cheddar cheese

½ cup yogurt, plain

1 teaspoon salt

Parsley for a garland

DIRECTIONS

Fry bacon, crumble.

Use olive oil and sauté onion approximately 5 minutes.

Stir in flour, approximately one minute extra.

Stir in stock until combined. Add milk and potatoes.

Cook until simmer. Reduce heat and simmer until potatoes are done.

Can add cheese or yogurt, salt and pepper to taste, and parsley as a garland.

Contributed by Dr. Connie Swenty

Taco Salad

INGREDIENTS

1 pound hamburger

2 large tomatoes

Small jar taco sauce

1 cup shredded cheddar cheese

1 green pepper

1 bunch green onions

Small bottle Russian dressing

1 small bag Doritos tortilla chips

1 head lettuce

DIRECTIONS

Brown hamburger and drain.

Chop tomatoes, pepper, and green onions.

Add to taco sauce, Russian dressing.

Add hamburger and cheese to mixture.

Add Doritos (crush, not fine in bag). Add head lettuce and mix.

Contributed by Leola Bragg

Tomato Basil Soup

INGREDIENTS

1 (15 ounces) can petite diced tomatoes

2 (8 oounces) can tomato sauce

1 carton chicken broth

1 Tablespoon minced garlic

1 Tablespoon basil

1 whole onion, finely chopped

Salt and pepper to taste

2 ½ cups heavy cream

1 ½ cups shredded Parmesan cheese

DIRECTIONS

Pour all ingredients into a crockpot.

Cook for 4 hours on low.

When cooking is finished, pour in 2 ½ cups heavy cream and 1 ½ cups shredded Parmesan cheese.

Stir until thickened.

Serve Hot

Contributed by Nancy Tappe and June Linn

Tomato Tortellini Soup
From Rolla Daily News

INGREDIENTS

3 Tablespoons of olive oil

¼ teaspoon crushed red pepper (optional)

1 cup of diced yellow onion

2 cloves garlic, minced

4 cups of broth

2 cans crushed tomatoes

2 Tablespoons basil, fresh chopped

1 teaspoon Italian seasoning

1 teaspoon salt

½ teaspoon of pepper

¾ cup of cream

1 bag of tortellini

2 cups of fresh spinach or kale

Parmesan cheese, grated

DIRECTIONS

Add olive oil to large soup pot, and bring to simmer over medium heat. Add red peppers and onion. Sauté. Stir in garlic and cook for one minute.

Add broth and tomatoes. Bring to a boil. Stir in basil, Italian seasoning, salt and pepper, sugar. Simmer for 30 minutes.

Let cool. You can use a blender and puree until smooth if desired, the return to soup pot.

Add cream and simmer over low heat for 10 minutes.

Stir in tortellini. Cook 5 – 8 minutes until thoroughly cooked.

Stir in spinach. Cook 2 – 3 minutes until wilted.

Taste to adjust seasoning.

Top with Parmesan before serving.

Contributed by Dr. Connie Swenty

Spiral Noodle Pasta Salad

INGREDIENTS

1 box gluten-free spiral noodles

Combine:

½ green bell pepper, diced

½ red bell pepper, diced

½ onion, diced

1 apple, diced

½ cucumber, diced

Set aside.

Dressing:

1 Tablespoon mustard

4 Tablespoons lime juice

2 Tablespoons olive oil

1 Tablespoon ketchup

1 Tablespoon soy sauce

3 Tablespoons mayonnaise

Pinch of salt and pepper

DIRECTIONS

Boil gluten-free spiral noodles, drain, set aside. When slightly cooled, add 2 Tablespoons olive oil and combine to keep from sticking.

Combine well.

Combine diced mixture with dressing and pour over pasta.

Mix well.

Add 1 can of tuna and mix well.

Contributed by Deidra Holtmeyer

World's Best Buttermilk Ranch Dressing

INGREDIENTS

1 cup mayo (Hellman's)

½ cup buttermilk

1 teaspoon Accent

1 teaspoon dill week

½ teaspoon garlic powder

½ teaspoon onion powder

1 Tablespoon dry parsley

¼ teaspoon salt

¼ teaspoon pepper

DIRECTIONS

I use a Mason jar to make this, but any sealable container will work.

Put the wet ingredients in first to the powders don't stick to the bottom.

Wet first, then dry.

Shake well.

Place in fridge for at least 30 minutes (overnight is best)

Shake well before each use.

Store in refrigerator for up to 1 week.

!! YUM !! Put it on everything!

Contributed by Kent Craighead

Meats and Main Dishes

Baked Noodles in Parmesan Sauce

INGREDIENTS

1 package of egg noodles

1 stick butter

2 cups Half N Half

1 teaspoon salt

1 teaspoon pepper

1 ½ cups Parmesan cheese

½ cup Mozzarella cheese, shredded

2 teaspoons lemon juice

DIRECTIONS

Boil Egg Noodles

Butter a 9 x 13 baking dish

In a Large Skillet, melt butter.

Add Half N Half

As it thickens, add salt, pepper, cheeses, and lemon juice.

Pour over noodles and pour into baking dish.

Bake at 350 degrees for 10 – 12 minutes.

Contributed by Marsha Light

Baked Peppers with Meat – Sharon Style

INGREDIENTS

4 green peppers

1 pound ground port

1 pound ground beef

2 small cans tomato sauce

Diced onion and garlic

Salt and pepper to taste

2 Tablespoons brown sugar

2 cups cooked rice

1 - 2 cups shredded cheese

DIRECTIONS

Preheat oven to 350 degrees.

Brown pork and beef together in skillet.

Add onion, garlic, salt, pepper, tomato sauce and brown sugar.

Cup peppers in half. Grill in pan on top of stove.

In a baking dish, place peppers face up, and add rice over them.

Add meat sauce over that, then cheese.

Cover dish with foil and bake for 20 minutes.

Serve with mashed potatoes!

Contributed by Sharon Warren

Beachcomber Casserole

INGREDIENTS

2 pounds ground beef

1/8 teaspoon black pepper

1 cup chopped onion

1 cup chopped green pepper

1 ½ teaspoon slat

1 package (8 ounces) shell small macaroni

1 can whole kernel corn, drained

1 Tablespoons lard or drippings

½ cup chopped ripe olives

¾ cup chopped pepperoni

2 cans (10.5 ounces) condensed tomato soup (or spaghetti sauce)

DIRECTIONS

Preheat oven to 350 degrees.

Cook shell macaroni according to directions on package and drain.

Brown meat, onion, and green pepper in lard or drippings.

Combine meat mixture, salt, pepper, macaroni, corn, tomato soup, and ripe olives.

Place in a 2 ½ quart casserole dish. Bake for 30 minutes.

Contributed by Leola Bragg

Chicken Packets

INGREDIENTS

2 - 3 cups cooked deboned chicken (skin removed and cubed)

3 ounces cream cheese

2 Tablespoon milk

3 Tablespoon butter

1/8 of an onion (sauteed in the butter above)

1 package of crescent rolls

½ cup parmesan cheese

DIRECTIONS

Allow butter and cream cheese to stand until room temperature.

Sauté onion in butter.

Combine the cream cheese and milk. Blend well.

Add sauteed onions and chicken to mixture.

Pinch 2 squares together at the perforated edges to make the rectangles as shown below.

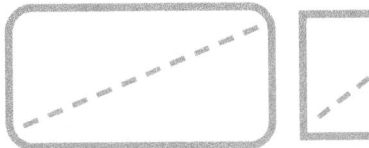

Add 2 Tablespoons of the chicken mixture on top of the rectangle. Fold over and seal the edges.

Bake in 350° oven until golden brown. Approximately 20 - 25 minutes. Very good!

Contributed by Pat Wagoner

Chow Mein

INGREDIENTS

2 celery stalks

1 whole onion

4 cups water

1 pound ground beef

1 pound ground pork (or two pork chops)

½ bottle Soy sauce

Salt to taste

Pepper to taste

2 Tablespoons cornstarch

1 cup cold water

1 can sliced water chestnuts (optional)

1 can bean sprouts (optional)

1 can sliced mushrooms

DIRECTIONS

Pour water into pot, heat over stove to boiling. Add celery and onions.

In a fry pan, cook the hamburger and pork. Drain and set aside.

In a cup of water, briskly stir in cornstarch.

When celery is softened, thicken with cornstarch mixture.

Add in meat and vegetables. Season with pepper, salt and soy sauce.

Serve over a bed of chow mein noodles and a side of rice.

Contributed by Nancy Tappe and June Linn

Crock Pot Ranch Pork Chops

INGREDIENTS

6 – 8 pork chops or small package of pork steaks

1 can cream of chicken soup

1 package dry ranch dressing mix

DIRECTIONS

In crock pot, layer pork chops, add cream of chicken soup.

Then sprinkle dry ranch dressing all over.

Cover and cook on high for 4 hours or low for 6 hours.

The pork chops come out very tender and the flavor is amazing.

You also get a good gravy for mashed potatoes.

Contributed by Deidra Holtmeyer

Hamburger Stew

(This recipe was dated March 18, 1934)

INGREDIENTS

1 ½ pounds hamburger

Medium onion, diced

3 large potatoes, diced

Carrots, diced

Salt and pepper to taste

1 can mushroom gravy

DIRECTIONS

Cook hamburger, onions, and salt, pepper.

Add carrots and potatoes.

Cover with water.

Cook until done, then add gravy and blend well.

Enjoy!

Contributed by Lolita Martin

Lebanon Summer Sausage

INGREDIENTS

5 pounds ground beef

1 cup dry milk

3 ½ Tablespoons salt

2 teaspoons onion powder

1 teaspoon allspice

1 Tablespoon paprika

2 teaspoons garlic powder

1 teaspoon coriander

1 Tablespoon white pepper

1 cup ice water

3 Tablespoons Liquid Smoke

DIRECTIONS

Mix dry milk, salt, onion powder, allspice, paprika, garlic powder, coriander, and white pepper. Set aside.

Mix ice water and Liquid Smoke. Set aside.

Stir together and add the ground beef. Refrigerate the mixture for 24 hours.

Remove from refrigerator and stuff into casings.

Place in a preheated smoker and smoke until the temperature reaches 155 degrees.

Remove from the smoker and mist with cool water.

NOTE: Ground wild game may be substituted for the beef.

Contributed by Sharon Tennyson

One Pot Beef Roast and Vegetable Dinner

INGREDIENTS

3 – 5-pound beef roast (chuck, sirloin tip)

5 Tablespoons all-vegetable shortening

1 medium onion, peeled and cut I slices or chopped

3 Tablespoons minced garlic

½ teaspoon salt

1 teaspoon pepper

1 ½ cups water

8 medium sized white potatoes, peeled and quartered

12 carrots, peeled and cut in half

DIRECTIONS

Melt the shortening in a large cast iron Dutch oven. Place onion slices in Dutch oven and cook until softened and slightly brown. Add garlic and stir together.

Salt and pepper the roast and sear on all sides in the Dutch oven.

Add water, cover the Dutch oven, and cook 30 minutes.

Add potatoes and carrots and continue cooking until vegetables are tender.

NOTE: You may need to add water while cooking if water evaporates too quickly.

Contributed by Mary Lina Grisham and Jacqueline Grisham

Party Meatballs

INGREDIENTS

Meatballs:

3 pounds ground beef

2 eggs

2 cups Quick Oats

2 teaspoons salt

1 teaspoon pepper

1 cup chopped onions

1 can (13 ounces) evaporated milk

1 teaspoon garlic powder

2 Tablespoons chili powder

Sauce for Meatballs:

2 cups catsup

½ teaspoon garlic powder

2 cups brown sugar (not packed)

½ cup chopped onion

2 Tablespoons Liquid Smoke

DIRECTIONS

Preheat oven to 350 degrees.

Mix thoroughly the ingredients for the meat balls.

Shape ¾" – 1" balls.

Place on pan in single layer.

Mix together ingredients for sauce and pour over meatballs.

Bake approximately 1 hour.

Quantity: 100 servings

Contributed by Mary Rosenburg

Sloppy Joes

INGREDIENTS

- 2 pounds ground beef
- 2 medium chopped onions
- 2 – 3 minced garlic cloves
- 2 cups ketchup
- 1 cup BBQ sauce
- 2 Tablespoons vinegar
- 2 Tablespoons prepared mustard
- 1 teaspoon Italian seasoning
- 1 teaspoon onion powder
- 1 teaspoon salt
- 1 teaspoon pepper
- 2 Tablespoons brown sugar

DIRECTIONS

Cook the beef, onions, and garlic over medium heat until done, breaking into crumbles.

Stir in ketchup, BBQ sauce, vinegar, brown sugar, mustard, Italian seasoning, onion powder, salt, and pepper.

Reduce heat and simmer for 20 minutes.

Contributed by Sharon Tennyson

Steak Marinade

INGREDIENTS

½ cup olive oil

¼ cup Worcestershire sauce

2 cloves smashed garlic

2 Tablespoons Montreal Steak Seasoning

1 Tablespoon red wine vinegar

½ teaspoon dried basil

½ teaspoon Italian seasoning

2 pounds of steak

DIRECTIONS

Mix all the ingredients together except steak.

Place in a Ziploc bag.

Add steak.

Marinate for several hours.

Contributed by Sharon Tennyson

Stuffed Peppers

Low Carb recipe
From Online: Kalyn's Kitchen

INGREDIENTS

1 TBLS olive oil

20 ounces of Italian sausage or turkey sausage

1 pound ground beef

Salt and pepper

1 small onion, diced

2 Table minced garlic

3 cups cabbage

2 TSP diced basil

2 tsp dried oregano

4 large red/green bell peppers

½ cup Parmesan cheese

¾ cup mozzarella cheese, grated

DIRECTIONS

Heat oven to 350 degrees.

Spray dish with non-stick spray or olive oil.

Brown meat, season with salt and pepper.

Chop onion and shred cabbage.

Brown onion and cabbage.

Add basil and oregano to cabbage.

Turn off heat. Mix in meat and cheeses

Stuff peppers.

Bake 30 minutes at 350 degrees.

Top with more cheese after baking for 30 minutes.

Bake 30 more minutes.

Contributed by Dr. Connie Swenty

Tuscan Chicken

INGREDIENTS

2 cans chicken soup (undilated)

2 cups Half and Half

2 teaspoons Tuscan Italian seasoning

2 cups Monterrey Jack cheese (divided)

1 cup Parmesan cheese (divided)

1 pound package linguine cooked per to package directions

4 cups cubed cooked chicken

½ teaspoon salt

¼ teaspoon pepper

½ teaspoon garlic powder

DIRECTIONS

Preheat oven to 350 degrees.

In a large bowl, combine soup, Half and Half, 1 cup Monterrey Jack cheese, 1 cup Parmesan cheese, Tuscan Italian seasoning, salt, pepper, and garlic powder.

Stir in the linguine and cooked chicken.

Transfer to a 4-quart baking dish. Sprinkle the remaining cheese on top.

Bake uncovered for 30 – 45 minutes or heated through.

Contributed by Sharon Tennyson

Zucchini Casserole

INGREDIENTS

6 - 8 cups cubed zucchini (unpeeled if small; if large, peel and seed)

¼ cup onion

1 cup shredded carrots

1 teaspoon salt

1 can cream of chicken (or mushroom) soup

¾ can milk in the soup can

8 ounces sour cream

8 ounces box of seasoned stuffing mix

1 pound sausage (regular or hot), fried, drained

Shredded cheese (if desired)

DIRECTIONS

Cook zucchini, onions, and carrots in salted water about 5 minutes. Drain.

Fry sausage, drain off fat.

Combine soup, milk, and sour cream; stir well. Fold in zucchini mixture and sausage. Add stuffing mix, stirring well.

Spray a 9" x13" baking pan with cooking spray. Pour mixture into pan.

Bake at 350 degrees for 25 minutes.

Add shredded cheese and bake 5 minutes to melt. Enjoy!

NOTE: I have amended this recipe many times and many ways. If I need a smaller casserole, I only use the 6 cups. You really cannot put too much zucchini in it. I use seasoned cornbread stuffing mix. I have included milk to make it moister. To peel the zucchini, I use a potato peeler and scoop out the seeds with a spoon. It makes it easier and faster!

Contributed by Pat Wagoner

Side Dishes

Barbecued Sauerkraut
(This recipe is different, but good)

INGREDIENTS

½ cup chopped onion

1 can (16 ounces) sauerkraut, drained

¾ cup brown sugar

7 strips bacon, cut up

1 can (16 ounces) tomatoes with juice and cut up

DIRECTIONS

Preheat oven to 350 degrees.

In a small skillet, fry onions and bacon together.

In a 2-quart casserole dish, combine sauerkraut, tomatoes, and brown sugar with bacon and onion.

Bake uncovered for 2 hours. Casserole should look caramelized around the edges.

5-6 servings.

Contributed by Leola Bragg

Cabbage Cheese Casserole

INGREDIENTS

Cabbage, cut into small pieces

Salt to taste

Cheese Sauce:

½ stick oleo

1 Tablespoon flour

4 slices cheese (add more if you wish)

1 ½ cup milk

DIRECTIONS

Cook Cabbage for 10 minutes. Drain. Place in baking dish.

Cook Cheese Sauce and add to the cabbage.

Bake for 30 minutes.

Add cracker crumbs on top.

Contributed by Leola Bragg

Cabbage Casserole

INGREDIENTS

Medium size head of Cabbage

6 slices bacon

Medium onion, chopped

¾ cup milk

½ cup mayonnaise

1 can celery soup (undiluted)

1 cup shredded cheese

1 cup breadcrumbs

DIRECTIONS

Preheat oven to 350 degrees.

Chop medium size head of cabbage and pre-cook I until slightly tender. Drain very well.

In a skillet, cook bacon to crisp.

Brown onion in bacon grease.

Crumble bacon and add onion and bacon to cabbage, along with milk, mayonnaise, and celery soup.

Pour into 9" x 13" pan.

Add shredded cheese, then top with breadcrumbs.

Bake until bubbly, approximately 25 minutes.

Contributed by Mary Rosenburg

Cheese Cauliflower

INGREDIENTS

Cook 1 head of cauliflower

Cheese Sauce:

2 Tablespoons butter

2 Tablespoons flour

1 teaspoon dry mustard

¼ teaspoon salt

Dash of pepper

½ cup milk

1 cup (4 ounces) American cheese

DIRECTIONS

Melt butter. Blend in flour, mustard, salt, and pepper.

Cook over low heat, stirring constantly until smooth and bubbly.

Remove from heat.

Stir in milk. Heat to boiling, stirring constantly. Boil and stir 1 minute.

Stir in cheese. Cook on low heat until cheese is melted.

Contributed by Lolita Martin

Cheesy Hash Browns

INGREDIENTS

1 package shredded hash browns

1 can cream of chicken soup

2 cups shredded cheddar cheese

¾ cup sour cream

¼ cup chopped onion

¼ cup melted butter

Topping:

1 ½ cup crushed Corn Flakes

2 Tablespoons melted butter

DIRECTIONS

Heat oven to 350 degrees.

Spray a 2 quart glass baking dish with nonstick cooking spray.

In a large bowl, combine first 6 ingredients. Mix well. Spread into prepared baking dish.

In a small bowl, stir together topping ingredients. Spread topping evenly over hash browns.

Bake 45 minutes or until has browns are tender.

Contributed by Leola Bragg

Corn Casserole

INGREDIENTS

1 can whole kernel corn

1 can creamed corn

1 egg

8 ounces cream cheese

1 packages Jiffy Cornbread Mix

1 stick oleo

DIRECTIONS

Preheat oven to 350 degrees.

Melt oleo in a 9" x 13" baking dish.

Mix all ingredients remaining ingredients.

Add mixed ingredients to oleo and bake for 45 minutes.

Contributed by Leola Bragg

Creamy Cauliflower Bake

INGREDIENTS

1 head cauliflower

1 teaspoon garlic, finely chopped

¼ cup onion, finely chopped

1 (8 ounces) package cream cheese

1 cup Parmesan cheese

Green onion tops chopped for garnish

1 teaspoon rosemary

½ teaspoon salt

¼ teaspoon pepper

DIRECTIONS

Preheat oven to 325 degrees.

Add water to an 8-quart pot and bring to boil.

Add cauliflower and cook over medium heat until softened (not too soft).

Drain, then pour cauliflower into casserole dish.

Mix the remaining ingredients except cheese in a microwave safe bowl and melt until softened.

Pour over cauliflower. Top with cheese.

Bake covered for 1 hour.

Garnish with green onion tops.

Serve hot.

NOTE: Any cheese can be substituted for Parmesan.

Contributed by Nancy Tappe

Hot Yeast Rolls

INGREDIENTS

1 cup sugar

2 packages active dry yeast

1 ½ cups warm water

3 well-beaten eggs

4 ½ - 5 cups plain flour

½ cup shortening

2 teaspoons salt

Melted butter

DIRECTIONS

Dissolve yeast in ½ cup warm water. Let stand 10 minutes.

Combine the yeast, eggs, 2 ½ cups flour, water, shortening, sugar, and salt.

Beat until smooth at medium speed.

Using a wooden spoon, stir in remaining flour to make a soft dough.

Cover and let rise until doubled.

Punch down dough and make into rolls.

Allow rolls to to rise to double in size.

Bake at 400 degrees for about 12 – 15 minutes.

Brush with melted butter when done.

Contributed by Sharon Tennyson

Houston House Rolls

INGREDIENTS

1 quart warm water

½ cup lard

2 teaspoons baking powder

1 cake yeast

1 teaspoon salt

1 teaspoon baking soda

Flour

½ cup sugar

Melted butter

DIRECTIONS

Dissolve yeast in water. Add salt, sugar, and lard. Mix well.

Put baking soda and baking powder in a flour sifter. Sift into the other ingredients.

Add enough flour to make a soft dough.

Roll a small quantity of dough at a time 1" thick.

Brush top with melted butter.

Fold over and cut with biscuit cutter. Prick each roll with a fork and brush with melted butter.

Put into baking pan and let rise for 30 minutes in a warm area.

Preheat oven to 350 degrees.

Bake about 15 minutes until lightly brown.

Makes approximately 100 rolls.

NOTE: Houston House was a hotel located in Newburg, Missouri many years ago and served family size meals, and these rolls were always served and people loved them.

Contributed by Mary Rosenburg

Perfect Dill Pickles

INGREDIENTS

Cucumbers

Dill

2 pods of garlic per jar

1 Tablespoon sugar per quart jar

13 cups water

1 cup salt

6 cups vinegar

DIRECTIONS

Pack cucumbers into jars with a sprig of dill and garlic.

Add 1 Tablespoon sugar to each quart jar.

Do not boil the sugar.

Boil the water, salt, and vinegar for 15 minutes.

Pour the brine over the cucumbers filling the jars to the top. Seal tight.

Set the jars in boiling water deep enough to cover the jars and let jars stand until cool.

Contributed by Sharon Tennyson

Scotch Eggs

INGREDIENTS

4 eggs, hard boiled, peeled

1 egg, beaten

1 pound breakfast sausage, bulk

1/3 cup flour

½ teaspoon salt

¼ teaspoon black pepper

2 ounces breadcrumbs

DIRECTIONS

Mix flour, salt, and pepper.

Make four even patties with sausage.

Roll the eggs in the flour mixture and then cover with sausage. Be careful to encase each egg completely.

Roll in the flour mixture and set upright by flattening the end of the egg.

Roll the eggs in the beaten egg and then breadcrumbs.

Either deep fry for 5 minutes or place on cookie sheet and bake for 30 minutes at 400 degrees.

Serve with mustard.

Contributed by Jacqueline Grisham

Shoepeg Corn Casserole

INGREDIENTS

2 cans (11 ounces each) shoepeg or white corn, drained

1 can (10 ¾ ounces) condensed cream of celery soup (undiluted)

1 cup (8 ounces) sour cream

1 cup shredded cheddar cheese

1/3 cup chopped onion

½ cup chopped celery

¼ cup green pepper

¾ cup butter flavored crackers (crushed) – about 18 crackers

2 Tablespoons melted butter

DIRECTIONS

Preheat oven to 350 degrees.

In large bowl, combine first seven ingredients.

Transfer to greased 2-quart baking dish.

Sprinkle with cracker crumbs.

Drizzle with butter.

Bake uncovered for 20 – 25 minutes or until bubbly.

Contributed by Mary Rosenburg

Apple Crumb Pie

INGREDIENTS

Crust:

1 (9-inch) unbaked pastry shell

-OR-

1 ½ cups sifted flour

½ teaspoon salt

½ cup shortening

4 – 5 Tablespoons cold water

Filling:

5 – 7 tart apples (5 cups)

½ cup sugar

¾ teaspoon ground cinnamon

Crumb Topping:

2/3 cups sugar

1 ½ cups all-purpose flour

1 ½ sticks softened butter

Contributed by Jeannie Feller

DIRECTIONS

Crust:

Preheat oven to 400 degrees.

Mix flour and salt. Add shortening. Use a fork or pastry blender to combine. Add cold water 1 Tablespoon at a time.

Knead the crust into a ball. Roll thin with rolling pin.

Filling:

Pare apples. Core and cut in eighths. Arrange in unbaked pastry shell.

Mix sugar and cinnamon. Sprinkle over apples.

Crumb Topping:

Combine sugar, flour, and butter until crumbly. Sprinkle over apples.

Bake for 40 minutes or until done. Cool.

Serve topped with ice cream or Cool Whip.

Apple Dapple Cake

INGREDIENTS

3 cups flour

1 teaspoon baking soda

1 teaspoon salt

2 cups sugar

3 eggs

1 ¼ cups oil

2 teaspoons vanilla

3 cups chopped apples

1 ½ cups chopped nuts

Topping:

1 cup brown sugar

1 stick butter

¼ cup milk

1 cup chopped pecans

DIRECTIONS

Preheat oven to 350 degrees.

Mix together sugar, eggs, oil, and vanilla.

Stir flour, baking soda, and salt together. Add to wet ingredients.

Fold in apples and nuts. Mixture will be very stiff.

Bake for an hour in a greased and floured tube pan. Do not remove cake from the pan until it is cooled.

Mix topping ingredients together, cook for 3 minutes, and pour over warm cake.

Contributed by Sharon Tennyson

Banana Nut Bread

Moist and Delicious!

INGREDIENTS

½ cup softened butter

1 cup sugar

2 eggs

3 bananas

2 cups flour

1 tsp baking soda

½ teaspoon salt

½ cup chopped walnuts (optional)

3 Tablespoons buttermilk

DIRECTIONS

Preheat oven to 325 degrees.

Mash bananas in a medium bowl. Set aside.

Cream sugar and butter in mixing bowl. Add eggs and bananas.

In another bowl, mix flour, baking soda and salt.

Alternate mixing flour mixture and milk into creamed sugar bowl. Stir until well incorporated.

Add in nuts and pour into greased bread pan.

Bake for 1 hour. Cool on wire rack.

Contributed by Nancy Tappe

Blackberry Cream Cheese Pie

INGREDIENTS

8 ounces cream cheese, softened

¼ cup sugar

1/8 teaspoon salt

1 egg

1 Tablespoon lemon juice

2 pre-make refrigerated pie crusts

1 large can of blackberry pie filling

2 Tablespoons sugar for sprinkling

DIRECTIONS

Preheat oven to 400 degrees.

Mix cream cheese, sugar, salt, egg, and lemon juice until smooth.

Place 1 pie crust in pie pan.

Put mixture in pie pan and bake for 20 minutes.

Remove and reduce oven temperature to 350 degrees.

Gently add can of pie filling on top of cream cheese mixture.

Place last pie crust on top of pie or you can lattice the top pie crust.

Sprinkle lightly with sugar.

Bake an additional 20 – 25 minutes until top crust is lightly browned.

Serve.

Contributed by Jacqueline Grisham

Blackberry Dessert

INGREDIENTS

Crust:

2 sticks butter

1 ½ cups flour

Filling:

8 ounces cream cheese, softened

¾ cup sugar

¼ cup milk

Topping:

1 ½ cups sugar

½ cup water

4 cups blackberries

6 Tablespoons cornstarch

12 ounces whipped topping

Chopped nuts (optional)

DIRECTIONS

Preheat oven to 350 degrees.

Melt butter and mix well with flour. Press into 9" x 13" baking dish.

Bake for 20 minutes. Cool.

Mix the filling ingredients together and pour over cooled crust.

For the topping, mix together sugar, water, blackberries and cornstarch in a medium saucepan.

Bring to boil and cook 3 minutes. Cool.

Once cool, pour on top of cream cheese layer, and spread evenly.

Top with whipped topping.

Add chopped nuts if desired.

Refrigerate.

Serves 12 – 16.

Contributed by Leola Bragg

Chocolate Chip Cookie Dough to Eat Raw

INGREDIENTS

1 cup butter, softened (2 sticks melted)

1 cup white sugar

1 cup packed brown sugar

½ cup water

2 teaspoons vanilla

3 cups all-purpose flour

½ bag chocolate chips

DIRECTIONS

Open 2 sticks of butter and put in large glass measuring cup. Put in microwave, add a few drops of water, and put paper towel over top to stop splashing as it melts.

Melt for 90 seconds or until melted completely.

Add water, white and brown sugar, vanilla, and flour. Mix thoroughly.

Let sit a few minutes until it cools a little.

Stir in half a bag of chocolate chips.

Serve and enjoy!

Contributed by Dr. Kitty Bickford

Coconut Cream Cake

INGREDIENTS

1 package white cake mix

¼ cup vegetable oil

1 ½ cups water

2 eggs

2 cups flaked coconut

8 ounces cream of coconut (mixed well)

8 ounces Cool Whip

DIRECTIONS

Preheat oven to 350 degrees.

Combine cake mix, oil, water and eggs. Beat for two minutes with an electric hand mixer. Add one cup of coconut flakes and mix well.

Pour batter into a greased 9"x13" baking pan and bake for 30 – 40 minutes.

Remove from oven and while the cake is still warm, poke holes in the cake with a large-tined fork. Pour cream of coconut over the cake and cool.

Spread Cool Whip over the cake and then sprinkle with the remaining 1 cup coconut flakes. Serves 12.

Contributed by Sonia Gibbs

Coffee Punch

INGREDIENTS

12 cups strong coffee

1 cup sugar

2 teaspoons vanilla

½ gallon chocolate milk

½ gallon vanilla ice cream

DIRECTIONS

Brew 12 cups of strong coffee.

Stir in sugar and vanilla.

Allow to cool slightly.

Pour into punch bowl.

Add chocolate milk. Chill.

Just before serving, add ice cream.

NOTE: Coffee and chocolate milk may be made the day before.

Contributed by Sharon Tennyson

Crack Cake

INGREDIENTS

1 box Duncan Hines Yellow Cake Mix

¼ cup brown sugar

¼ cup white sugar

1 box instant vanilla pudding

2 teaspoons cinnamon

4 eggs

¾ cup water

¾ teaspoon oil

½ cup white wine

DIRECTIONS

Preheat oven to 350 degrees.

Mix the above ingredients with blender.

Grease tube pan.

Pour into mold.

Bake for 1 hour.

When cake comes out of oven, melt 1 stick of butter in 1 cup sugar and ¼ cup wine.

Pour over hot cake.

Cool. Unmold onto plate.

Serve.

Contributed by Deidra Holtmeyer

Cranberry Chip Cookies

INGREDIENTS

1 cup butter, softened

1 cup sugar

2 egg yolks

1 teaspoon vanilla extract

2 ¼ cups all-purpose flour

½ teaspoon baking powder

¼ teaspoon salt

1 ½ cups chocolate chips

1 ½ cups dried cranberries

¾ cup chopped pecans

½ cup English toffee bits or almond brickle chips (optional)

DIRECTIONS

Preheat oven to 350 degrees.

In a large mixing bowl, cream butter and sugar. Add egg yolks and vanilla. Mix well.

Mix flour, baking powder and salt. Gradually add to the creamed mixture and mix well.

Stir in chocolate chips, cranberries, pecans, and toffee bits (if desired).

Drop by round Tablespoons, 2 inches apart, onto ungreased cookie baking sheets. Flatten slightly.

Bake for 11 – 14 minutes or until set and edges are lightly browned.

Cool, remove to wire racks.

Yields 6 dozen.

Contributed by Leola Bragg

Creamy Blueberry Gelatin Salad

INGREDIENTS

2 packages (3 ounces each) grape gelatin

2 cups boiling water

1 can (21 ounces) blueberry pie filling

1 can (20 ounces) unsweetened crushed pineapple (undrained)

Topping:

1 package (8 ounces) cream cheese, softened

1 cup sour cream

½ cup sugar

1 teaspoon vanilla extract

½ cup chopped walnuts

DIRECTIONS

In a small bowl, dissolve gelatin in boiling water. Cool for 10 minutes.

Stir in pie filling and pineapple until blended.

Transfer to 9" x 13" dish. Cover and refrigerate until partially set (about 1 hour).

For topping, in a small bowl, combine cream cheese, sour cream, sugar, and vanilla.

Carefully spread over the gelatin. Sprinkle with walnuts.

Cover and refrigerate until firm.

Contributed by Leola Bragg

Deluxe Oatmeal Raisin Cookies

INGREDIENTS

1 ¼ cup white, whole-wheat, or all-purpose flour

1 teaspoon baking soda

¾ teaspoon ground cinnamon

½ teaspoon salt

1 cup butter or margarine, softened

¾ cup sugar

¾ cup packed brown sugar

1 teaspoon vanilla extract

2 large eggs

3 cups quick or old-fashioned oats

11 ounces milk chocolate covered raisins

1 cup chopped nuts (optional)

DIRECTIONS

Preheat oven to 375 degrees.

Combine flour, baking soda, cinnamon, and salt in a small bowl.

Beat butter, sugar, brown sugar, and vanilla extract in a larger mixer bowl until creamy.

Beat in eggs; gradually beat in flour mixture.

Stir in oats, chocolate covered raisins, and nuts.

Drop by round Tablespoon onto ungreased baking sheets.

Bake for 9 – 11 minutes.

Cool on baking sheets for 2 minutes; remove to wire racks to cool completely.

Makes 4 ½ dozen.

Contributed by Jacqueline Grisham

Dessert Pizza

INGREDIENTS

1 roll sugar cookie refrigerated dough, softened

1 package (8 ounces) cream cheese

½ cup sugar

Fresh fruit: Strawberries, blueberries, kiwis, bananas, or whatever you enjoy

DIRECTIONS

Preheat oven to temperature on sugar cookie dough package.

Spread cookie dough by pressing it to fit pan.

Bake until golden brown. Cool.

Combine cream cheese and sugar, beat well.

Spread over cookie, then have fun making the pizza.

Chill for 1 hour.

Contributed by Sharon Warren

Easy Pineapple Casserole

INGREDIENTS

2 sticks oleo, melted

3 eggs, beaten

1 ½ cup sugar

1 can (16 – 20 oz) crushed pineapple (include juice)

8 slices toasted bread cubes

DIRECTIONS

Preheat oven to 350 degrees.

Mix together in a large baking dish and bake for 45 minutes.

Contributed by Leola Bragg

Easy Sugar Free Chocolate Pie

INGREDIENTS

1 (1.4 ounces) package of sugar free chocolate instant pudding

1 cup 2% milk

1 (6 ounces) ready to eat graham cracker crust

1 (8 ounces) container whipped topping

2 Tablespoons toffee and chocolate pieces

DIRECTIONS

Whisk together the instant pudding and milk until well blended.

Add in 1 cup of softened whipped topping until well blended.

Pour mixture into the graham cracker crust.

Top the pie with the rest of the whipped topping.

Sprinkle toffee and chocolate pieces over top of the pie to complete.

Refrigerate for one hour and serve.

Contributed by Tiffany McCormack and Jacqueline Grisham

Fruit Pizza

INGREDIENTS

1 package sugar cookie dough mix

1 tub cream cheese fruit dip

1 cup strawberries

1 kiwi

1 can Mandarin oranges

DIRECTIONS

Preheat oven to 350 degrees.

Line baking pan with parchment paper and lightly grease.

In a mixing bowl, make sugar cookie dough according to package directions.

Press dough evenly across a round baking sheet.

Bake until golden brown. Cool.

Top dough with fruit dip and spread evenly across the round baking sheet.

Slice strawberries and kiwis to desired size.

Place desired amount of fruit on top of the pizza, chill for 30 minutes to 1 hour, then serve.

Contributed by Elizabeth Veasman

Gluten-Free Orange Bundt Cake

INGREDIENTS

1 large orange, cut in small pieces

3 eggs

1/3 cup oil

½ cup sugar, plus 1 Tablespoon

Sift:

2 cups gluten-free flour

2 Tablespoons baking powder

Dash of salt

Glaze (if desired):

1/3 cup butter

2 cups confectioners' sugar

1 ½ teaspoon vanilla

4 Tablespoons hot water

DIRECTIONS

Combine and mix well and pour evenly over cake

In a blender, combine and blend orange and eggs. Add oil and sugar. Blend well.

Pour into bowl and add flour, baking powder and salt mixture.

Mix well. Batter should be thick, but if you think it is too thick, add 2 Tablespoons orange juice.

Transfer to greased baking pan and bake at 400 degrees for 40 minutes.

Ice with cream cheese icing or glaze if desired.

Contributed by Deidra Holtmeyer

Gluten-Free Oreo Bundt Cake

INGREDIENTS

13 ounces Gluten-Free Oreo Cookies

4 eggs

½ cup oil

1 cup milk

½ cup sugar

½ cup gluten-free flour

1 Tablespoon baking powder

DIRECTIONS

In a blender, add Oreo Cookies, eggs, oil, and milk. Blend well.

Pour into a bowl and add sugar and flour. Mix well. Add baking powder. Mix well.

Butter and flour Bundt pan. Pour in mixture and bake at 400 degrees for 35 minutes.

Eat plain or add your favorite icing. I use buttercream frosting.

You can make this recipe with regular Oreo Cookies and flour. This is one of the best gluten-free recipes ever! Very delicious.

Contributed by Deidra Holtmeyer

Hawaiian Cheesecake

INGREDIENTS

Crust:

½ cup butter, melted

1 ½ cups graham cracker crumbs

1/3 cup sugar

Filling:

8 ounces softened cream cheese

8 ounces whipped topping

1 large can (14-16 ounces) crushed pineapples, drained

¾ cup confectioners' sugar

½ cup pineapple chunks

½ cup shredded coconut (for topping)

DIRECTIONS

Crust:

Mix the graham cracker crumbs and sugar.

Add the melted butter and stir to combine well.

Pless into an 8" x 8" or 9" x 9" square pan.

Filling:

In a large bowl, beat the softened cream cheese and confectioners' sugar until very smooth.

Beat in the whipped topping. Then fold in the drained crushed pineapple.

Spread the filling on top of the crust.

Top with pineapple chunks and sprinkle with coconut.

Chill very well, at least 4 hours, preferably overnight.

Contributed by Sonia Gibbs

Lazy Man's Peach Cobbler

INGREDIENTS

1 stick butter

1 cup milk

1 cup sugar

1 cup flour

1 teaspoon baking powder

Dash of salt

1 quart sweetened peaches (or other fruit), drained

DIRECTIONS

Butter the bottom of an 8" x 8" baking dish.

Drain fruit and place it on bottom of the pan.

Pour milk over the fruit.

Mix all other ingredients and pour evenly over the top.

Bake at 350 degrees for approximately 45 minutes.

Sprinkle sugar on top and cook for 10 more minutes.

Contributed by Deidra Holtmeyer

Lucky 7 Pie Crust

INGREDIENTS

4 cups flour

1 Tablespoon salt

1 egg, well beaten

½ cup cold water

1 ½ teaspoons salt

1 ½ cup shortening

1 Tablespoon vinegar

DIRECTIONS

Blend flour, salt, and sugar.

Add shortening and cut in with a pastry blender.

Mix the egg, water, and vinegar. Add to flour mixture.

Don't overwork the dough or it will be tough instead of flaky.

Roll out the dough and shape into pie pan.

Contributed by Sharon Tennyson

Maple Syrup by Scratch

(This was my mother's recipe – Mary Grisham)

INGREDIENTS

1 cup sugar

1 cup brown sugar, packed

1 cup water

1 teaspoon maple flavoring

1 teaspoon butter flavoring (optional)

Pinch of salt

DIRECTIONS

Bring to a boil.

Add flavoring.

Makes a little over one cup.

For a large group to feed, double the recipe.

Delicious on your pancakes or waffles.

Contributed by Sharon Warren

Million Dollar Pie

(Recipe makes 2 pies)

INGREDIENTS

2 cooked pie crusts

1 can Eagle Brand Condensed Milk

1 can (20 ounces) crushed pineapple (juice included)

1 small box vanilla instant pudding

1 cup coconut

1 cup chopped nuts (pecans)

2 Tablespoons lemon juice

2 containers Cool Whip

DIRECTIONS

Mix the pineapple and pudding and milk until well blended.

Stir in remaining ingredients.

Pour into baked, cooled pie shells.

These are thick pies and very delicious, plus easy to make.

Contributed by Mary Rosenburg

Old Fashion Yellow Cookies

INGREDIENTS

½ cup butter, softened

1 ½ cups flour

½ teaspoon baking soda

¼ teaspoon salt

2 Tablespoons milk

1 cup sugar

1 teaspoon vanilla

1 egg

Chocolate chips (optional)

Nuts (optional)

DIRECTIONS

Preheat oven to 350 degrees.

Mix as for any cookie recipe.

Add chocolate chips, nuts, or anything you want, or leave plain,

Drop and bake for 8 – 10 minutes

Contributed by Mary Rosenburg

Orange Dream-Sickle Salad

INGREDIENTS

1 box orange Jell-o

1 box instant vanilla pudding

1 cup boiling water

½ cup cold water

8 ounces Cool Whip

14 ounces can mandarin oranges, drained

1 cup mini marshmallows

DIRECTIONS

Combine Jell-o and boiling water. Whisk until dissolved.

Add cold water and chill for 15 minutes in refrigerator.

Slowly whisk in vanilla pudding mix until smooth and chill for another 15-20 minutes or until slightly thickened.

Fold in Cool Whip, mandarin oranges, and marshmallows.

Contributed by Deidra Holtmeyer

Pastor Brian's Pumpkin Bars

INGREDIENTS

4 eggs, room temperature

1 2/3 cups sugar

1 cup canola oil

15 ounces canned pumpkin

2 cups flour

2 teaspoons Cinnamon

2 teaspoons pumpkin pie spice

2 teaspoons baking powder

1 teaspoon baking soda

1 teaspoon salt

Cream Cheese Frosting:

6 ounces cream cheese, softened

2 cups confectioner's sugar

¼ cup butter, softened

1 teaspoon vanilla

1 – 2 Tablespoons whole milk

DIRECTIONS

Preheat oven to 350 degrees.

Beat eggs, sugar, oil and pumpkin until mixed.

Combine dry ingredients and gradually add to pumpkin mixture.

Pour into an ungreased 9" x 13" baking dish.

Bake for 25-30 minutes.

Cream Cheese Frosting:

Mix cream cheese, confection's sugar and butter.

Add vanilla and 1 – 2 Tablespoons whole milk.

Frost when bars are cooled.

Pumpkin Pie Squares

INGREDIENTS

Crust:

1 cup flour

½ cup oatmeal

½ cup brown sugar

½ cup butter, softened

Filling:

1 can (16 ounces) pumpkin

1 can (13 ½ ounces) evaporated milk

2 eggs

½ teaspoon salt

1 teaspoon cinnamon

½ teaspoon ginger

¼ teaspoon ground cloves

Topping:

½ cup chopped pecans

½ cup brown sugar

2 Tablespoons butter

DIRECTIONS

Crust:

Preheat oven to 350 degrees.

Combine flour, oatmeal, brown sugar, and butter in mixing bowl on low speed.

Press into ungreased 9" x 13" baking pan. Bake for 15 minutes.

Filling:

Combine pumpkin, canned milk, eggs, sugar, salt, and spices; beat well. Pour into crust.

Bake for 20 minutes.

Topping:

Combine pecans, brown sugar, and butter. Sprinkle over pumpkin filling. Return to oven and bake for 15 – 20 minutes or until filling is set.

Cool in pan and cut 2" squares.

Makes 2 dozen.

Contributed by Leola Bragg

Red Velvet Crinkles

INGREDIENTS

1 box Red Velvet cake mix (16 ounces)

1/3 cup Canola or vegetable oil

2 large eggs

2 Tablespoons all-purpose flour

¼ teaspoon almond extract

1 cup sugar

DIRECTIONS

Preheat oven to 350 degrees.

Mix all ingredients together and chill until firm, about 2 hours.

Scoop into 1" balls. Roll in sugar.

Bake until the edges look dry.

Cool in pan for about 5 minutes. Ready to serve or store.

Contributed by Mary Rosenburg

Sopapilla Cheescake Bars

INGREDIENTS

2 Cresent Dough Sheets

2 (8 ounce) blocks of cream cheese, softened

1 cup sugar

¼ cup (4 Tablespoons) melted butter

1 teaspoon vanilla extract

Cinnamon sugar

DIRECTIONS

Preheat oven to 350 degrees.

Spray 9" x 13" baking pan with cooking spray.

Press 1 dough sheet into the bottom of the greased baking pan and bake for 6 minutes.

In a large mixing bowl, combine cream cheese, sugar, and vanilla extract.

Mix until smooth.

Spread out on the baked dough and cover with second dough sheet, pressing into the corners.

Brush melted butter over top of the dough then top with cinnamon sugar.

Bake for 30 minutes.

Contributed by Norman Veasman

Sweet Cinnamon Biscuits

INGREDIENTS

2 cups sifted all-purpose flour

1 Tablespoon baking powder

1 teaspoon salt

¼ teaspoon baking soda

¼ cup vegetable oil

¾ cup buttermilk

1 stick butter, softened

¼ cup sugar

1 teaspoon cinnamon

1 cup milk (optional)

DIRECTIONS

Preheat oven to 400 degrees. Lightly grease 9" round baking pan.

In a medium bowl, combine flour, baking powder, salt, and baking soda. Mix well.

Stir in vegetable oil. Add buttermilk and stir just until blended.

Knead the dough on a lightly floured surface until smooth. Roll dough into an 8" x 15" rectangle. Spread butter over the dough.

In a small bowl, combine sugar and cinnamon. Mix well. Sprinkle over butter.

Roll up the rectangle, jelly roll fashion, starting from the long side. Pinch seams to seal.

Cut the roll into 1 ½-inch slices. Arrange the slices cut side up in prepared baking pan.

Bake until lightly browned, 15 – 20 minutes.

Remove from oven. If desired, pour milk over the top.

Serve hot.

Contributed by Sharon Warren

Truffles

INGREDIENTS

8 ounces semi-sweet chocolate

8 ounces bitter-sweet chocolate

8 ounces meltable milk chocolate

1 can condensed milk

1 Tablespoon vanilla extract

Sea salt, nuts, and sprinkles (optional)

DIRECTIONS

In a double boiler, heat semi-sweet and bitter-sweet chocolate.

Add condensed milk. Stir until chocolate is melted. Continue to stir until it is a marshmallow texture.

Stir in vanilla.

Remove from heat.

Cool. Cover and refrigerate for 2 hours.

Once chilled, roll into balls, then roll in melted milk chocolate coating.

Sprinkle with sea salt, nuts, and sprinkles as desired.

Contributed by Sharon Tennyson

Zuccini Bread

INGREDIENTS

1 cup sugar

1 cup brown sugar

3 eggs

1 cup vegetable oil (you can substitute apple sauce for ½ the oil)

3 teaspoons vanilla

3 cups all-purpose flour

1 teaspoon nutmeg

1 Tablespoon ground cinnamon

1 teaspoon baking powder

1 teaspoon salt

1 teaspoon baking soda

2 cups zucchini

1 cup chopped walnuts (optional)

DIRECTIONS

Preheat oven to 325 degrees.

Grease two bread pans (or 6 mini loaf pans).

Mix flour, salt, baking powder, baking soda, nutmeg, and cinnamon in a bowl.

Beat eggs, oil, vanilla, and sugar in large bowl.

Add dry ingredients to egg mixture and stir until combined.

Grate zucchini. Stir into the mixture along with the nuts until well combined.

Pour into pans and bake 40 – 60 minutes (55 average), or 35 – 40 minutes for mini loaf pans.

Contributed by Jacqueline Grisham

Calvary Cherubs

Calvary's Cherubs Cook

Aidynn Noilges (Age 10)

I like to make pizza. I would make that with my Mom.

I would get out all the ingredients. She would just tell me.

I would help her take it out of the oven and put it in.

Then we would wait a little bit. We would be watching the Simpsons.

Then we would call my Sister, and we would sit down at the table to eat!

Lakota Moentmann (Age 8)

I like watermelon. With a grown-up, I can cook.

I would go to the store and get some hamburger and put it in a pan.

I usually do it with my sister. I don't know what else to say.

Echo Moentmann (Age 6)

I like chicken nuggets from McDonalds.

I would cook them in an air fryer.

I'd get them at Wal-Mart.

Then I'd take them out and eat them.

They are my favorite!

Also bacon. I love to eat bacon.

My Mom makes it for me. And sometimes my sister Misty.

Isaac Baggett (Age 11)

I like mac and cheese!

Add ½ cup then I'd use the box.

The I'd add ¼ cup milk, the 4 Tablespoons BUTTER.

Then I'd add the cheese packet from the box.

And then that's all the stuff you need.

And then the noodles of course.

Emma Hodge (Age 10)

I like cottage cheese, but I don't know how to make it.

I like buffalo wings, but I never made them before,
but I think I know how to.

I would buy chicken wings from Krogers.

I'd separate the wings from the rest of the body.

But I'd keep the done.

Then I'd dip it in Buffalo Sauce.

Then I'd dip it in breadcrumbs.

Then back in Buffalo Sauce.

Then cook it for 30 minutes or forever long you cook meat.

I think it is 30 minutes.

Then plate it and put Ranch on the side.

William Cottner (Age 4)

Chicken nuggets is my favorite thing to eat and I like French fries too!

You can make them in the microwave.

I make French fries in the oven.

I cook them on a pan.

I set the time to know when they are done.

Lilly Demire (Age 11)

My favorite thing to make is brownies.

I normally make them with my Sisters!

I get the box and read the instructions.

I mixed it. Then well, added 2 eggs.

Then I mixed it again.

Then I put it in a foil pan and baked it

For 10 minutes.

Cheryl Holtmeyer (Age 12)

My favorite thing to make is spaghetti.

Put sauce and noodles. Cook noodles first.

Then make meat into size of golfballs.

Cook the meatballs. Add sauce to meatballs

On top of noodles.

Put it all together.

Serve with garlic bread.

Just cook the toast with garlic and butter!

Aaron Hodge (Age 8)

Banana nut muffins are my favorite.

Bananas, nuts, and muffins are all you need.

Just ask my Mom, she will know.

Henry Mendenhall (Age 9 ½)

I like to make brownies.

Eggs, chocolate chips and brownie mix and maybe milk.

I don't know.

Harper Light (Age 9)

I like spaghetti.

Brown your hamburger in a pan.

Boil the spaghetti.

Add it together and add the sauce.

I would serve it with cheese bread and salad.

Cheese bread goes in the oven.

I put lettuce, tomatoes, cheese, and croutons on top of my salad.

Payton Light (Age 7)

I like to make hamburgers and fries.

I like to make my hamburgers on the grill.

And I make them, but Pop flips them for me.

For her fries, she cuts up her potatoes and cooks them in the fryer.

She says, "I like to sprinkle with salt and Parmesan."

Paisley Degroat (Age 7)

I like to eat spaghetti mostly!

So you have to start with spaghetti strings and then pizza sauce.

You have to put it in the microwave till it's warm or something.

And the you can add meatballs.

JESUS IS...

To the Artist	He is the Portrait of All That is Beautiful.
To the Astronomer	He is the Bright and Morning Star.
To the Acheologist	He is the Master Designer.
To the Builder	He is the Sure Foundation and Chief Cornerstone.
To the Banker	He is the Unsearchable Riches of God.
To the Baker	**He is the Bread of Life.**
To the Carpenter	He is the Plumb Line of Perfect Righteousness.
To the Doctor	He is the Great Physician.
To the Electrician	He is the Light of the World.
To the Florist	He is the Lily of the Valley and the Rose of Sharon.
To the Farmer	He is the Lord of the Harvest.
To the Geologist	He is the Solid Rock on Which We Stand.
To the Homemaker	He is the Door.
To the Insurance Man	He is not a piece of the rock. He IS The Rock.
To the Jeweler	He is the Pearl of Great Price.
To the Kitchen Chef	**He is the Recipe of Righteousness.**
To the Lawyer	He is the Righteous Judge.

To the Mother	He is the Compassionate Son.
To the Minister	He is the Word of God and the Message of Hope.
To the Newspaperman	He is Good Tidings of Great Joy – Born to you a Savior.
To the Optometrist	He doesn't improve sight – He gives sight.
To the Pharmacist	He is the Balm of Gilead.
To the Philosopher	He is the Wisdom of God.
To the Preacher	He is the Good News of God for a world gone bad.
To the Queen	He is the King.
To the Restless	He is the Giver of Peace, Joy, Hope, and Home.
To the Religionist	He is the Way of Relationship with God.
To the Student	He is the Great Teacher.
To the Slave	He is the Master.
To the Servant	He's the Lord.
To the Statesman	He is the Prince of Peace.
To the Traveler	He is the Way.
To the Theologian	He is the Author and Finisher of Our Faith.
To the Thirsty	He gives the water of life, and they shall never thirst again.
To the Undertaker	He is the Up-Taker!
To the Victim	He's the Victor!

To the Wounded	He is the Lord God who heals infirmities.
To the Sinner	He is the Lamb of God who takes away the sin of the world.
To the Saint	He is Jesus Christ, Son of God, Savior, Redeemer, Friend.

By Pastor Rick Ousley

www.ingramcontent.com/pod-product-compliance
Lightning Source LLC
Chambersburg PA
CBHW081500070526
44586CB00019B/2441